Explaining Deliverance

Sharing experience
in the ministry of deliverance

Graham Dow
Bishop of Carlisle

with a Foreword by
Simon Barrington-Ward
former Bishop of Coventry

Sovereign World

Sovereign World Ltd
PO Box 777
Tonbridge
Kent, TN11 0ZS
United Kingdom

Unless otherwise indicated, all scripture quotations are from the New
International Version, inclusive language version, copyright the
International Bible Society 1999; published by Hodder and Stoughton.

ISBN: 1 85240 334 9

The publishers aim to produce books which will help to extend and build
up the kingdom of God. We do not necessarily agree with every view
expressed by the author, or with every interpretation of Scripture expressed.
We expect each reader to make their judgment in the light of their own
understanding of God's Word and in an attitude of Christian love and
fellowship.

Typeset and printed by CRB Associates, Reepham, Norfolk
Cover by CCD, www.ccdgroup.co.uk
Printed in the United States of America

Preface to the Second Edition

This booklet is offered primarily for the increasing number of Christians in our churches who are persuaded of the reality of evil spirits and who seek guidance as to how to practice deliverance ministry. For those who need a more detailed explanation, I have addressed the grounds for believing in demons in a separate paper.* I also recommend Graham Twelftree's *Christ Triumphant*, an extension of his Nottingham University doctorate on the subject of Jesus the Exorcist.

Since I wrote the First Edition of this booklet, the former Jesuit priest, Francis MacNutt has published *Deliverance from Evil Spirits*. Francis has a wealth of experience in the ministries of healing and deliverance and covers the subject admirably. He deals with whether or not demons really exist, explains how he first became involved with this ministry, and gives instruction on how to pray for deliverance.

Some may be concerned that a booklet such as this gives Satan too much attention. I thoroughly sympathize with this view as I have no interest in glorifying Satan. However, in a short booklet on deliverance ministry it is not possible to cover the necessary ground without looking closely at Satan's work.

In this Second Edition, chapter four has been rewritten for the sake of clarity. There is also substantial extra material in

---

* "The Case for the Existence of Demons" in *Churchman* 94, 3 (1980) pp. 199–208, now available from Graham Dow at Rose Castle, Dalston, Cumbria CA5 7BZ. Please send a stamped addressed envelope (booklet size) and 50p payable to Graham Dow.

chapter 5 to clarify the theological truth that gives a firm basis for the faith necessary to bring about deliverance. Otherwise, the content of the booklet remains much as in the first edition with only minor adjustments.

Suggested further reading

Cuming, G.J., *Hippolytus: A Text for Students* (Grove Liturgical Study no. 8, 1976)

Dow, Graham, *The Local Church's Political Responsibility* (Grove Pastoral Series no. 2, Cambridge, 1996)

Horrobin, Peter, *Healing through Deliverance: the biblical basis* (Sovereign World, Tonbridge, 1991)

MacNutt, Francis, *Deliverance from Evil Spirits* (Chosen Books/ Baker, Grand Rapids, 1995)

McAll, Kenneth, *Healing the Family Tree* (Sheldon, 1982), especially chapter 3

Mitton, Michael and Parker, Russ, *Requiem Healing* (Daybreak, London, 1991)

Mitton, Michael, *The Quick and the Dead* (Grove Pastoral Series no. 32, 1987)

Perry, Michael (ed. on behalf of the Christian Exorcism Study Group) *Deliverance* (SPCK, 1987)

Powell, Graham, *Christian Set Yourself Free* (Sovereign World, Tonbridge, 1986)

Richards, J. *Exorcism, Deliverance and Healing* (Grove Booklet on Ministry and Worship no. 44, third ed. 1990)

Subritzky, William, *Demons Defeated* (Sovereign World, Tonbridge, 1986)

Twelftree, Graham, *Christ Triumphant* (Hodder, London, 1985)

Wagner, C.P., ed., *Territorial Spirits,* (Sovereign World, Tonbridge, 1991)

Acknowledgements

I am indebted to those who read the manuscript for the first edition and made many helpful comments. This includes Bishop Simon Barrington-Ward, David MacInnes, Audrey Martin-Doyle, Bishop David Pytches, and all the members of the Grove Pastoral Group at the time of writing the first edition. I also wish to express my warmest gratitude to the people of Holy Trinity Church, Coventry. They lovingly gave me freedom to share and teach amongst them and were willing for the journey of taking risks, making mistakes, and learning together.

Contents

Foreword

by

Simon Barrington-Ward

former Bishop of Coventry

I shall never forget living and ministering in a Nigerian student hostel at Ibadan University, and spending my first holiday there in a Nigerian village. This had a radical impact on my approach to combating evil. I had to learn new ways of praying, preaching and teaching.

Having traveled since in Africa and Asia and having stayed with people in the churches there, I have realized what a significant learning experience that was. The sense of the powers of evil at work in the daily detail of life is common to many cultures outside our own. Moreover, books like the psychiatrist M. Scott Peck's *People of the Lie, the Hope for Healing Human Evil* are beginning to seriously examine the phenomena of evil in our own society.

When I first came across Graham Dow's approach to these issues here in the midst of our Western culture, I felt uncertain quite how to respond. At the very least I was impressed enough, as I trust readers of this book will be, to want to look carefully, and discover what I had to learn.

While I still do not feel entirely at home with Graham's approach, I have already gained a great deal from it, as from so many other aspects of his ministry. I would therefore urge the most skeptical reader to suspend disbelief and explore seriously what Graham is opening up to us. At the very least, within this language and style of approach, there are lessons for all of us.

One of the most important of these is the way in which Graham demystifies "evil spirits," even if he refuses to demythologize them. His treatment of them must so reduce them in scale and significance as to disclose them to be a manageable nuisance and nothing more. This takes a great deal of the sting out of the fears and fantasies of any who have attributed too much to such causes. It reduces the exotic significance of the occult and the bizarre, so fashionable in many quarters today.

Graham's work shows us that in this area, as in so many, *"perfect love casts out fear."* A sane faith in God's love in Christ delivers us from every kind of evil within and without, in whatever form we understand it to take. It is this sense of peace and proportion about Graham's whole approach which gives it its own weight. I am grateful to him for his ministry and for his book.

1

Introduction and examples

This booklet is offered as one minister's experience in the field of deliverance ministry from evil spirits. It is the result of a journey. Whereas some years ago I believed that the presence of evil spirits in a person in the Western world is rare, I now believe that such spirits are widespread. In my judgment most of them are not powerful and can be dealt with straightforwardly. They easily pass undetected in a culture which does not believe in their existence.

I take the commonplace presence of evil spirits to be in agreement with the worldview of reality indicated in the Gospels of Matthew, Mark and Luke. Here the driving out of evil spirits is treated as routine. It is practiced in close association with a healing ministry, as the kingdom of God is announced by Jesus. In our twenty-first century I would want to see the ministry of deliverance take its place as a normally routine and unspectacular ministry, alongside prayer for healing, confession, counseling, medical and psychiatric help, each form of knowledge making its own contribution to the healing process.

Equally important, in my own understanding, is the ministry of healing through changing society. I developed that theme in my booklet, *The Local Church's Political Responsibility*.

It is only the so-called developed Western countries which have difficulty with belief in evil spirits. The majority of the world is quite used to understanding them as part of reality. The question there is not "Do they exist?" but "Who has power over them?"

The dean of a Chinese theological college, visiting the diocese of Coventry in a Mission in Partnership exercise in 1988, roared with laughter when I told him that most English clergy do not believe in evil spirits. We should be open to the possibility that the rest of the world is right in its perception of the way things are.

"Why should we accept a 2,000-year-old worldview today?" I am sometimes asked. The answer I give is that the New Testament view of spiritual reality should at least be considered without prejudice. We should simply see whether or not it makes better sense of what we experience today than the interpretative models commonly used in our society.

In my experience, even among Christians, this open and unprejudiced hearing is rarely allowed. This indicates that we are afraid of the possibility of evil spirits – they are unthinkable to us. Or perhaps their existence is acceptable, provided that they are only rarely encountered! Behind this there is a far-reaching cultural prejudice against both the supernatural and whatever is outside our human control. We do not like the idea of unseen spiritual powers influencing our lives.

We are glad to believe in God insofar as he provides us with an explanation for the world and a help in time of trouble. We are not so disposed to the belief that we are accountable to him. People believe in a supernatural God to the extent that it suits them. When it comes to the Spirit of God, the devil or demons, however, it is another matter. To expect that the Spirit of God may act powerfully with a tangible presence, like breath or wind, is worrying to us. We like to know that we are in control.

Yet all the time people are having experiences of transcendence which challenge us to be aware of the Spirit of God. For some it is a beautiful sunset, for others listening to choral music, or walking through a cathedral. Somehow people know that there is someone greater than human life and are aware of his presence. Many have no language for speaking of these experiences of the majesty of God.

On the dark side, people have experiences of a sense of evil: for example, in certain rooms or buildings, or when face to face with a certain person. Again our culture gives no language with which to speak of the spiritual forces they are encountering. As a society we have been bankrupt in our understanding of spiritual things, but there are signs that this is changing. The Christian church is learning again to welcome the Holy Spirit's power as a vibrant reality in daily experience, and so also we are becoming more open to the possibility of evil spirits. In short, we are regaining our belief in spiritual power.

The church also has a long tradition of consecrating its churches. Many ministers are also asked from time to time to bless houses and sometimes to deal with what is sensed as the presence of evil in a house. There seems to be an intuitive sense amongst people that there is such a thing as the sacred presence of God and that there can also be unholy presences.

Since spiritual reality is not open to empirical observation, arguments for the existence of spirits are difficult to confirm or deny. We can neither prove nor falsify the existence of evil spirits, any more than we can the existence of God or angels. If we are going to know the answer it will be through revelation from God, through both the scriptures and the natural order. This revelation can be confirmed through our experience and in the consistency of reason.

"But how can a loving God allow a realm of invisible spirits to affect us?" is the sort of question still uppermost in some people's minds. This is actually a key to understanding the whole problem of evil in God's world. To believe in rebellious, fallen angels (Jude 6; Revelation 12:9) is not, in principle, more difficult than to believe in human beings' free will to rebel and sin.

God, in his wisdom, has allowed a world in which we have been given the choice between right and wrong. Consequently we are able to do immense harm to one another. Yet we can also learn to love and care for one another and choose what is right. Moreover, as Christians we have the power of Christ to resist evil, in ourselves and others.

Some examples of deliverance

Linda

Linda is a strong and stable person with no indication of psychological disturbance, yet she discovered as she grew up that she had unsought occult powers. She had pre-knowledge about when people were going to die, which numbers had won raffles, and when certain people were coming in her direction although they were still out of sight. She was also attracted to books on witchcraft and as she read them knew that she had powers by which she could do the things described in the books. She experienced strong irrational opposition within her to Christian leaders, wanting to harm them.

We discerned the presence of evil spirits inherited from the practice of witchcraft in earlier generations. Deliverance was accomplished gradually over several years. It took time partly because of my inexperience, but more particularly because of the need for Linda to come to the point where she was totally resolved to renounce the powers she inherited and bring her will completely into submission to Jesus Christ. She did not find it easy: her occult experiences had been part of her for the whole of her life and to discard them seemed to be to lose something of her own self.

Tony

We met Tony when he was a student. While we were praying for emotional healing and security in Christ, we affirmed that he was God's child and that his home was in heaven. Quite suddenly his voice said, "No, it is not." It was a demonic spirit within him speaking. Marked physical manifestations of the presence of a spirit repeatedly followed in his eyes, face and body.

Several areas of sin were renounced, step by step, including sexual behavior and his interest in films such as *The Exorcist*, but the spirit stubbornly refused to depart. Several prayer sessions were held. Eventually Tony was willing to face the possibility of inherited powers and admitted to seeing violence in his father.

A murdering power was discerned, and when challenged the spirit said, "You've found me."

Deliverance was slow for two reasons. First, there was a problem in discerning the nature and origin of the leading spirit. Tony was reluctant at first to discuss the clues to inherited spirits as seen in his parents' behavior. Second, we began to see that although he could speak easily of a faith in Christ, the reality behind this was shallow and there was a lack of deep conviction and repentance. The time over which deliverance took place enabled a far deeper faith to be developed.

Frances

Frances became a Christian when studying for a professional qualification. However, when she got married a strange desire to despise and verbally attack her husband became apparent, a desire that she did not wish to have. I knew that her mother was a dominant, controlling person who had once gone for three years without speaking to her husband. I also knew that there was always one member of the family with whom the mother was not communicating. This indicated that Frances had inherited a spirit which was now attacking her relationship with her husband.

As we prayed, we became aware of witchcraft rituals and devil worship in Frances' ancestry. In the final ministry time Frances, and the two people praying for her, independently received through spiritual gifts pictures of a black stone, a ritual chalice, and the words "devil worship." It transpired that her grandmother had practiced fortune telling. Renouncing these acts proved hard for her, but eventually managed to do this, calling "Jesus, help me." As we gave her Holy Communion, something in her desired to attack me, but deliverance was finally accomplished and the spirits were thrown out. The irrational desire to attack her husband had completely gone.

Some years later she wrote:

Since then my life has been much the better. We have a very good marriage. My relationship with my mother is quite different, and no longer do I fear being "the one out of favor." Everything is much improved, including my own self-image.

Mary

Mary came forward at a conference for prayer in response to this word from the Lord: "There is someone who is longing to find hope for the future." Her husband had died nearly ten years earlier and she had become increasingly desperate. Even from her childhood years she had little enthusiasm for life and had almost looked forward to death.

Without knowing anything about Mary, through the Holy Spirit I discerned a spirit of abandonment. This coincided exactly with how she had felt in the months before the conference.. We believe that it entered from her father who was an 18-year-old raw recruit in the First World War and, like thousands of others, felt completely abandoned during and after the Battle of the Somme. This led him to have a major breakdown after the war.

Mary was set free from the spirit of abandonment and from a spirit of death. She wrote:

> I still cannot get over how different I feel. I feel a new person, and I believe in one sense I am! I feel loved and accepted by God more than ever before.

Seeing some of the same marks in one of her children she has subsequently met with others in prayer and sought to bring a similar release to him.

Please note the names of the people in these examples have been changed. Also, although two of these particular examples involved witchcraft in previous generations, this does not mean that witchcraft is always involved.

2

Deliverance ministry in the New Testament

It is important to see how deliverance ministry is shown to us in the Bible, particularly in the Gospels and Acts.

Dealing with spirits was routine ministry for disciples

Far from being told by Jesus that dealing with evil spirits is a ministry requiring specialist skill, the first disciples were given instructions to cast out spirits and heal every disease (Matthew 10:1; Mark 6:7, 13). Both deliverance and healing were seen as an integral part of announcing the arrival of the kingdom of God (Matthew 9:35).

When Jesus had called the Twelve together, he gave them power and authority to drive out all demons and to cure diseases and he sent them out to preach the kingdom of God and to heal the sick.
(Luke 9:1–2)

Jesus did not say, "If you come across an evil spirit take great care; report to me before proceeding." The impression, rather, was that dealing with evil spirits was as common and routine as dealing with sickness (though not to be confused with sickness). It follows then, that the ministry of deliverance can be handled by all Christian disciples acting with Christ's authority.

17

Deliverance is distinct from healing

Jesus did not treat all disorders as the result of evil spirits, and treated apparently similar conditions as on some occasions requiring deliverance and on other occasions not. Contrary to what has been argued elsewhere, the writers of the New Testament did not interpret disorders in demonic terms simply because such was the prevailing perception in their day. While a dumb and blind person was cured by deliverance (Matthew 12:22–23) and a dumb person similarly (Matthew 9:32), laying on of hands with no hint of deliverance from spirits is used for a dumb man (Mark 7:32–37) and a blind man (Mark 8:22–25).

It was in fact quite well known in the ancient world that mental disorder could rise from organic or psychological causes and it was not necessarily attributed to demonic causes. Examples can be found in Herodotus' *History* (2.173.4; 6.84.1) and Hippocrates' *On the Sacred Disease* (Chapters 1, 17, 18). In *Christ Triumphant*, Graham Twelftree refers to the critical stance of Josephus, Philo and Lucian towards supernatural claims.

Demons and spirits are the same thing

In Mark 6:7–13 it appears that the evil (in the Greek this is literally *"unclean"*) spirits over whom the twelve are given authority are the same as the demons they cast out on their mission. Similarly, the spirit in the Syro-Phoenician woman's daughter is called both an unclean spirit (Mark 7:25) and a demon (v. 29).

Again:

> *When evening came, many who were demon-possessed* [Greek: *demonized*] *were brought to him, and he drove out the spirits with a word and healed all the sick.*   (Matthew 8:16)

Spirits are invisible supernatural forces

Both the Old Testament Hebrew and New Testament Greek

words used for spirit are the same as those used for breath and wind, indicating real but invisible power. The Holy Spirit is compared to wind (John 3:8). When Jesus gives his Spirit to the disciples he breathes on them (John 20:22). I find it helpful to think of most evil spirits as rather like bad breath in a person.

Throughout the Gospels there is no hint of spirits which are good, other than the Holy Spirit, and there is no indication that Jesus allows spirits to remain in a person when the kingdom of God draws near. The presence of spirits is best described as "having" spirits; it is unhelpful to speak of people being "possessed" by a spirit or demon.

The various descriptions used in the Gospels and Acts are:

- *to be demonized* (many references; badly translated as *"possessed by a demon"*)

- *having a spirit* (a dumb spirit – *"a spirit that has robbed him of speech,"* Mark 9:17; *"an evil spirit,"* Mark 7:25; *"evil spirits,"* Acts 19:13; a spirit by which the person foretold the future, Acts 16:16; *"a demon,"* Luke 4:33)

- *a man with a spirit* (Mark 1:23)

- *being driven by the demon* (Luke 8:29)

- *many demons had gone into him* (Luke 8:30)

- *it seizes him* (Mark 9:18)

- *troubled by evil spirits* (Luke 6:18)

- *tormented by evil spirits* (Acts 5:16).

"Demonized" or *"having a demon"* certainly does not necessarily have the implication of being taken over by the demon, a concept which we understand by the word *"possessed."* In my judgment we should speak of people having spirits rather than being possessed.

Demons or spirits are of varied strength

The variety of language used for demonic involvement indicates varied degrees of affliction by these spirits. The usual word for a demon in the New Testament is the diminutive word *daimonion*, meaning something having either divine or demon-like attributes. In the popular understanding of the day, these were not always considered to be evil, nor were they necessarily thought to be particularly powerful. Their existence was simply accepted as part of the way things were.

The stronger word *daimon* is used in Matthew's account of the man whose spirits claimed to be legion (Matthew 8:31). The variation of the word suggests that spirits were thought to exist in varying strengths. In Luke's account the trouble afflicting the man is variously described in the account as demons, the demon, the unclean spirit (Luke 8:27–36). The variation between singular and plural suggests several spirits but one particular one as key to the deliverance.

Driving out spirits is part of liberating people from Satan's rule

The Gospels and Acts present the coming of Jesus as a battle in which the rule of God comes to set people free from the rule of God's enemy, Satan. Jesus himself said *"if I drive out demons by the finger of God, then the kingdom of God has come to you"* (Luke 11:14–23), and *"should not this woman, a daughter of Abraham, whom Satan has kept bound for eighteen long years, be set free on the Sabbath day from what bound her?"* (Luke 13:16).

In Acts 10:38 we read, *"God anointed Jesus of Nazareth with the Holy Spirit and power, and ... he went around doing good and healing all who were under the power of the devil, because God was with him."*

Although Satan is in no way the equal of God, at the present time he is the *"prince of this world"* (John 12:31; 14:30; 16:11). Because of that, *"your enemy the devil prowls around like a roaring lion looking for someone to devour"* (1 Peter 5:8). Satan was actually in a position to offer Jesus all the kingdoms of the world (Matthew 4:8–9).

Luke 11:14–23 portrays deliverance as a struggle for dominance between two strong men. Since it is a power struggle, it is not surprising to read that Jesus used more than one command to release the man in whom powerful spirits called themselves legion (Luke 8:29, 31). The disciples on at least one occasion failed to effect deliverance at all (Matthew 17:14–16). The good news is that Jesus secured final victory at the cross (John 12:31). We believe that at every level he sets people free to enjoy the peaceful rule of God. Sins are forgiven, bodies are healed, relationships put right, righteousness and justice spring up, and evil spirits are thrown out as the kingdom of God arrives. Paul declared that Jesus had sent him to the Gentiles *"to open their eyes and turn them from darkness to light, and from the power of Satan to God"* (Acts 26:18).

There is wide agreement amongst scholars that the Gospel passages are substantially authentic in reflecting the words of Jesus. It would be difficult to set them aside without destroying the understanding which Jesus seems to have had of his purpose on this earth.

Jesus threw out the spirits with a command

Graham Twelftree (*Christ Triumphant*, p. 96) writes:

> From data both within and outside the New Testament there is no doubt that Jesus was an exorcist – a very successful exorcist. Jesus never used the formula "I exorcise you by the Spirit of God." Instead he said "I command you [to come out . . .]" showing clearly that he thought he was acting on his own authority while being endowed with the Holy, eschatological Spirit.

The use of the Greek word *ekballo*, "I drive out" (e.g. Luke 11:20) confirms that Jesus with his own authority confronted an enemy frustrating the purpose of God in his people. On occasions shouting, screaming or strong physical movements accompanied the departure of the spirits (Mark 1:26; 9:26; Luke 4:33–36, 41).

The disciples commanded spirits in the name of Jesus

"Lord, even the demons submit to us in your name!"
(Luke 10:17)

"In the name of Jesus Christ I command you to come out of her!"
(Acts 16:18)

The Gospels and Acts show us that the disciples did their healing ministry as they had seen it modeled by Jesus, except for the additional invocation of his name (Acts 3:6; 9:34).

Twelftree convincingly shows in *Christ Triumphant* (pp. 96–99) that Luke wrote his two-volume work (the Gospel and Acts) so as to show the close parallels between the Holy Spirit at work through Jesus and the Holy Spirit at work through the Apostles. The continuity is clear. It is the same ministry of Jesus who began to do and teach things during his lifetime and continues now to do it through the church (Acts 1:1–2).

This means that we can read the accounts of Jesus' ministry as a model for our own practice rather than just as the wonder works of the divine Son of God. However, not all who remind us that Jesus was human as well as divine are agreeable to following the models of his healing and deliverance ministry practice.

We must contend against a range of unseen spiritual powers

Outside the Gospels and Acts we have further indications of the spiritual reality which lies behind the presence of evil spirits. Paul wrote:

> *Put on the full armor of God so that you can take your stand against the devil's schemes. For our struggle is not against flesh and blood, but against the rulers* [archas – "hierarchies"], *against the authorities* [exousias], *against the powers of this*

dark world [kosmokratores – "world controllers"] *and against the spiritual forces of evil in the heavenly realms.*

(Ephesians 6:11–12)

This language indicates that the battleground for the Christian is not primarily with human factors in opposition to Christian life, but with a range of unseen evil spiritual powers. The words used give clues that these powers operate in a hierarchy from Satan and seek to exercise controlling authority over human life. This understanding of reality is related to the Jewish belief at the time of Jesus that individual nations were associated with specific angelic powers in the heavens.

Further light is shed on this by the book of Revelation. In chapter 12 Satan appears in the imagery of heads, horns and crowns (Revelation 12:3). In the following chapter, similar horns, heads and crowns are ascribed to a beast to which Satan gives his throne and great authority (Revelation 13:2). This beast rules with power, persecuting Christians, and is understood as the Roman Empire, and, in particular, the emperor, Nero, coming to life again (see G.B. Caird, *The Revelation of St John the Divine*, Black, London, 1966, p. 162).

Here in picture form the truth is expressed that heavenly powers of evil operate through human power groups. A second demonic beast follows the first, supporting its authority (Revelation 13:11, 12) and later called the false prophet. This imagery shows Satan putting his authority onto human institutions or leaders when they embrace evil. While the interpretation of such symbolism is never a straightforward matter, here is further biblical evidence to support the view that unseen spiritual powers of evil are a reality with which we have to deal.

3

The New Testament view and our understanding today

It is often argued that Jesus was a man of his time and therefore interpreted sickness in terms of evil spirits. However, we have already noted that Jesus exercised discrimination, treating similar conditions as on some occasions requiring deliverance and on other occasions not.

Further, Jesus showed himself well able to disagree with other prevailing interpretations of his day. For example, he declared that sickness was not necessarily due to sin (John 9:1–3); that children were to be treated with significant status in relation to receiving the things of God (Mark 10:13–16); and that forgiveness could be pronounced with God's authority by his anointed representatives (Mark 2:5–11).

It is true that the understanding of the world as affected by Satan or demons is a late Jewish doctrine developed in the Hellenistic period. But so also is the doctrine of life after death which Jesus also taught and to which we cling eagerly! It is impossible to separate Jesus' references to Satan and demons from his understanding of his own mission, proclaiming the arrival of the rule of God and breaking the enemy's hold over the world.

No one has yet offered any adequate criteria by which we might decide which aspects of Jesus' teaching we should set aside as culturally determined and which not. Without such criteria we simply follow the accepted plausibility structures (right or wrong) of our own Western culture and these in themselves are inadequate grounds for dismissing those of the New Testament.

I have personally picked up evil spirits in a way that taught me of their reality. Some years ago I prayed with a woman to set her free from a fear of cancer. I did so with an air of self-confidence rather than a sense of dependence upon God. It happened that at this time my wife's father was dying with cancer. From the moment of that prayer I could not control my thoughts about cancer. It was as if my head took off. I had to put all thought of my father-in-law right out of my mind since I could no longer handle such thoughts rationally. I would not have believed this possible had it not happened to me. I asked someone with experience to cast the spirit out and then I was fine.

On another occasion I picked up a spirit that made me choke when taking Communion services. Neither of these spirits was very powerful but they hindered my Christian life and I am very glad to be free of them.

"Does it matter if we believe in evil spirits?"

If we fail to believe in evil spirits, we will be unable to correctly diagnose the cause of a problem when an evil spirit is present. This commonly leads to failure to release the person from the power of that spirit. I am doubtful if such release and freedom would have come to the people with whom deliverance ministry is described in chapter 1 by any other professional discipline.

Of course, there are also dangers in holding such beliefs. Just as those who spend a lot of time in hospital see a great range of human disorder and are liable to forget just how well the human condition develops its own immunity and protection to disease, so consciousness of the widespread presence of evil spirits is liable to make one forget the power of normal Christian worship to drive their presence away. Confession of sin, prayer and worship, the sacraments of the church and Christian obedience to God all play a vital part in protecting believers from the attack of spirits and also in setting them free.

It is as difficult to attest the existence of angels as of demons. Yet angels are mentioned three hundred times in the Bible. They are described as *"ministering spirits sent to serve those who will inherit salvation"* (Hebrews 1:14). Angels have a long and glorious tradition in Christian worship, theology and art. But if we choose to doubt the existence of evil spirits, we must realize that the case is no stronger for angels to exist.

"Surely a Christian cannot have an evil spirit?"

From my own experience I am quite certain that a Christian can have an evil spirit. Perhaps the wrong use of the word "possessed" has been the trouble here. We know that Christians are united with Christ at the center of their beings, yet sin still remains in us. It no longer rules us but it presses in on us. According to James, when we allow ourselves to be enticed by an evil desire, it *"gives birth to sin; and sin, when it is full-grown, gives birth to death"* (James 1:13–15).

In a similar way Christians who have an evil spirit find it pressing in on them; it influences the will, just as our sinful thoughts and desires affect the will to do what is right. The influence may only appear on certain occasions. I have heard the presence of a spirit likened to the malaria parasite, that is to say, it seems as if the disorder it creates only erupts at certain times.

Deliverance should be in partnership with other ministries

I do not argue that deliverance ministry is the be-all-and-end-all of healing ministry or even that it should be dominant. My hope is that it will be allowed to take a routine place in partnership with other ministries. I hope for the day, for example, when Christian ministers in partnership with physicians and psychiatrists can learn together in mutual trust when and how deliverance prayer can be effective. But this will require openness to explore its truth as a means of healing.

4

Clues to recognizing the presence of evil spirits

I offer this chapter cautiously, but on the basis of twenty-five years' experience of the ministry of deliverance. It is offered as a guide and not as an exhaustive or authoritative treatment of the subject. Here are clues to bear in mind when considering whether or not evil spirits are present. Some of the descriptions may rightly indicate evil spirits on some occasions, but not others. Some may be completely mistaken.

There is a danger of seeing spirits everywhere. However, I am prepared to risk making mistakes in order to open up possibilities that may not have been thought of, and which, when tried, may lead to effective ministry. In this unfamiliar area our understanding is very limited and we have much to learn.

Evil spirits live in the realm of darkness

Evil spirits live in the realm of sin, of rebellion against God. Only when there is room in a person for such darkness do the spirits have any right of entry. Therefore, persistent sin, deliberately doing what is not pleasing to God, is an invitation to the powers of darkness to enter. Their nature is to create disorder and to ruin human lives: they can cause or reinforce any kind of disaster.

A spirit can be identified by the particular disorder it relates to. Some evil spirits have names, for example, "a spirit of false gods."

Entry through sin comes in three main ways

Our own sin

Spirits enter a person through common areas of sin such as violence, occult practice, sexual sin and false worship. They come through well-embedded wrong attitudes such as anger, hate, bitterness or unforgiveness. The sin may be knowingly committed. It may also be committed in ignorance that such an action or attitude is sin, as, for example, with some occult practice, with fear, or a sense of rejection.

Sin done to us

God has created us to be people living together. We can, therefore, affect one another deeply by our words and actions. If we believe the cruel words people say to us, even just a little, that act of believing may give the bad statement or wish power in our lives. This is a kind of curse: the words are given power over us by a spirit.

Another example of a spirit entering through sin done to us is when someone abuses us, for example, with rape, violence or dominance. It may be the fear in us that offers an entry point.

Sin of previous generations

It should not surprise us that spiritual power, both good and evil, travels from one generation to another. We are beings created to be full of God's Spirit. As with every other part of our nature, an inheritance is handed on to our children. This is not a problem provided we take responsibility to make sure we pass nothing evil on.

It may be necessary to seek the ministry of deliverance ourselves or to seek wise and gentle prayer for our children to whom we might already have passed something on. The good news is that the Holy Spirit's positive presence also passes to the next generation.

Since there is little awareness in the Western churches of the reality of evil spirits and the churches have lost the art of deliverance, spirits have been passed on down family lines for many generations and their unholy presence has remained in houses or places where serious evil occurred in past generations.

Common entry points for evil spirits

False worship

All worship reaching out to transcendent beings or powers involves the spirit realm. There is no other channel that links earth and heaven. Whenever prayers and worship are offered that are not in accordance with the truth of God and Christ Jesus, a link is made with spirits of untruth and their presence are invited. Unfortunately, this is not widely realized.

Other religions

Paul said to the pagan Athenians that God purposed that people would seek to find him in different ways (Acts 17:26, 27). But since God has now revealed himself in the resurrection of Jesus as the one true Lord, he commands people everywhere to repent (Acts 17:30–31).

The world religions bear many statements about God and human destiny that do not agree with Christian truth. The confession of these statements in prayers and religious acts has the effect of opening the door to spirits of these religions.

It is also well known that astrology and other occult practices play a major part in several Eastern religions, indicating the association of these religions with the realm of evil spirits. Whenever prayers are said that are not "in truth," evil spirits may be present.

It may be that the early Christian Church had a wiser understanding of the hold of spiritual evil than we do in our own day. The early third-century document *Apostolic Tradition*, in the liturgies of Hippolytus, records that all baptism candidates took part in prayers for deliverance from evil spirits. This would be a strange thing to do if conversion to Christ was all that was needed to bring deliverance from the presence of any evil. It seems that the early Christians knew that new believers could bring darkness with them from other religions.

Cults

Modern-day cults which deny that Jesus is the true God and died for our sins carry spirits of deceit. Freemasonry, for example, eliminates Jesus from its prayers and gives God the name Jah-Bul-On (a combination of the name Yahweh with the pagan deities Baal and Osiris). Its Emulation Ritual states that "by square conduct, level steps and upright intentions we hope to ascend to those immortal mansions whence all goodness emanates." This is seeking salvation by morality, not by faith in the cross of Jesus Christ. The secrecy and unholy vows of Freemasonry all indicate its deception. I have once entered a Masonic temple and what was there did not agree with Jesus Christ in me.

Occult practice

Occult means "hidden." Occult practices, in general, seek knowledge through hidden powers either to find guidance, to bring about healing or to curse another person. At its most serious level, any past or present involvement in practices claiming to worship or serve the devil will certainly indicate the presence of evil spirits. Considerable psychological disorder is also likely.

It is important to note when a person shows an attraction to occult practices such as witchcraft, spiritualism, fortune telling and horoscopes, or to occult books, or shows an attraction to those who practice these things. The presence of spirits is probably indicated. Darkness seeks out darkness.

The presence of occult spirits is indicated also by superhuman strength or ability and by inexplicable knowledge other than that which clearly glorifies God. Such knowledge is often called "second sight." This is a difficult area since occult experiences of knowledge are counterfeit opposites of true words of knowledge from the Holy Spirit.

It is common in some societies. Writing as a Scot myself, I am aware through in-depth prayer ministry that some with Scottish ancestry may need deliverance from the residual power of appalling clan warfare and its atrocities in past generations. My suspicion is that most so-called "second sight" indicates more serious evil in previous generations, for example, curses with violence. Although the evil practice of the past has since been discarded, its power has not been fully broken.

This is another example of the way that evil spiritual power travels down generations until it is dealt with. "Second sight" is a kind of residue of spiritual power. I have met people born with powers of fore-knowledge which they never sought and yet which they felt gave them power over others. See the example of Linda in Chapter 1.

Some people view psychic powers as morally neutral, capable of being used for good or evil. The use of the word "psychic" in this context is unfortunate because, according to the Bible, the *psyche* or soul is a good and created aspect of our humanity, through which we share in all human relationships and open ourselves to God. The word "psychic" as used today, however, is about hidden spiritual powers which are liable to be the work of evil spirits unless clearly operating in obedience to Jesus Christ and his Holy Spirit.

Some occult activities such as Ouija boards are commonly considered harmless, but it is foolish to play the devil's games even for fun. Just as those who come to church for a "laugh" may be touched by the Spirit of God, so conversely it can be with activities which call upon spiritual powers that are not of God.

A woman came to see me who had committed her life to Christ many years earlier yet she had never had any sense of God's presence with her. I realized that something was blocking the Holy Spirit's ministry to her. The clue came when she shared that her father was of dogmatic religious opinions and was also hooked on horror films. In the name of Jesus I released her from this bondage inherited from her father and from whatever evil or occult practice lay behind it in previous generations. The presence of God came to her within minutes of this prayer.

This example shows the need to recover again the routine ministry of casting out spirits which Jesus gave to his disciples. Inherited spirits would then be dealt with whenever a person becomes a Christian.

Sin and wrong attitudes

Serious and deliberate personal sin is always liable to allow entry to evil spirits. Some common entry points are through sins of abortion, deceit, pornography, wrong sexual relationships, unwholesome sexual practices and body punishment.

Wrong attitudes often have very understandable causes. Nevertheless, to hold on to such an attitude rather than to repent and seek God's forgiveness is to take a completely contrary attitude to that taught in the scriptures. Here are some examples:

For if you forgive others when they sin against you, your heavenly Father will also forgive you. But if you do not forgive others their sins, your Father will not forgive your sins.

(Matthew 6:14–15)

But now you must rid yourself of all such things as these: anger, rage, malice, slander and filthy language from your lips. Do not lie to each other, since you have taken off your old self with its practices.

(Colossians 3:8–9)

"In your anger do not sin": Do not let the sun go down while you are still angry, and do not give the devil a foothold.

(Ephesians 4:26–27)

Do not repay evil for evil or insult with insult, but with blessing, because to this you were called so that you may inherit a blessing.

(1 Peter 3:9)

See to it that no one misses the grace of God and that no bitter root grows up to cause trouble and defile many.

(Hebrews 12:15)

Where wrong attitudes of bitterness and unforgiveness, of anger and hatred, are held in our hearts and not put far from us, they are simply an invitation to a demonic spirit. As we know, such attitudes are all too common, bringing darkness in families and even churches. One of the best routes to good health is to make sure that there is no one we have not fully forgiven. Wrong attitudes like this, especially when there is an evil spirit present, give rise to much illness. Sadly, people seek treatment for their bodily illness without attending to their spiritual dis-ease.

Traumatic events and oppression

I have already mentioned violence and rape and their potential to give entry to spirits. Other traumatic events include war, becoming a refugee, serious fires or accidents, bereavements and sexual abuse.

The emotions of shock and pain go very deep and make the human spirit very vulnerable to an evil spirit coming to reinforce the pattern of brokenness. The ground of entry for the spirit is the fear, shock or despair. While these responses are very understandable, they are not God's perfect will and there-fore bring darkness.

The history of trauma is more pronounced in some national-ities and communities than others. For example, I have found that deliverance prayer is important for some who have ancestors involved in mining. There is a history of ruthless exploitation, terrible conditions and pit accidents plunging families and whole communities into terrible grief. A measure of stubbornness and hardness has developed in reaction to what happened but was also present in the perpetrators.

Oppressive behavior takes many forms, all of which violate the dignity of another person or community. Attitudes of condemnation or rejection, for example, have power to affect us deeply. Finland is a nation which has been invaded by Russia fifty-three times, and the consequential sense of hurt and oppression in some of its people can open the door to darkness. This is why a nation's history is important in relation to the presence of evil.

I used to work in an area of London where many church

members were originally from the West Indies. They brought with them a background of West African voodoo and the evil practices of witch doctors. In addition, there was a history of slavery, which seriously affected models of behavior of manhood and womanhood. When most of the population became Christians, the churches lacked the understanding and skill to deal with spirits coming down the generations from past evil. Even in committed Christian people I have observed very strange behavior which I believe is traceable to the troubled history.

I am increasingly convinced that the spiritual hold related to such past events must be dealt with not only within individuals but also at corporate levels. Families, towns, churches and nations, for example, can all be affected. The story of a community is important in the sight of Jesus Christ as the letters to the Churches make clear (Revelation 2:1–3:22).

Ruling spirits

In the Old Testament four areas of sin are specified as bringing the land into pollution. They are:

- Idolatry (Jeremiah 3:1; 16:18)

- Bloodshed (Numbers 35:33)

- Occult practice (Deuteronomy 18:9–12)

- Sexual immorality (Leviticus 18:1–30)

It seems that serious sin gives evil some degree of ruling presence in a place. This will continue through the years and down the generations until it is dealt with.

Attention needs to be given to these powers and their effect on a house or family, a town or city, an organization, community, church or nation. Spirits which have gained a presence in a particular location are often called "territorial spirits." They can seriously block the progress of the gospel. Unlocking the history that has given rise to their presence is one of the recent insights in the work of evangelism.

Discerning evil spirits

Outward manifestations

The knowledge that someone is involved in any occult practice alerts us immediately to the probable presence of spirits contrary to Jesus Christ. Here are some other outward signs of the presence of evil spirits.

▶ *Reaction to Jesus*

Demons will not say that Jesus Christ has come in the flesh on earth (1 John 4:2–3) or that Jesus is Lord (1 Corinthians 12:3). By contrast, they will curse Jesus or deny him.

It must not be supposed that every person with an evil spirit will be unable to confess that Jesus Christ is Lord and incarnate. It is the spirit which denies the truth, not the person. The believer, with the presence of the Holy Spirit, will normally be able to confess Christ, although some difficulty may be experienced especially if the evil spirit is powerful. However, when a person shows pronounced difficulty in accepting the foundation doctrines of Jesus as taught by the church, it is possible that a spirit within them is affecting their ability to receive basic truths. This can shed light on difficulties a person may have, for example, in a confirmation or baptism class.

Second, demons resist the victory of the cross. In saying *"Get behind me, Satan!"* (Mark 8:33) Jesus recognized that it was not just Peter's human desires that were challenging his journey to the cross. Demons show a hostile and violent reaction in the face of the cross because it was there that they were defeated. One Christian leader I know recognized that she had a spirit when her lip curled as her minister used the cross on the altar to bring deliverance to another person.

▶ *Reaction to worship, prayer and holy things*

Demons react against the worship of God. Clues to their presence can be found in a person's restlessness or body movements during prayer or worship which seem in opposition to, rather than in harmony with, the Spirit.

It is not uncommon to find people who have an irrational reaction against Communion services and cannot explain why. This may indicate a spirit. Breaking Communion vessels, defacing Bibles and churches, and blasphemy are more blatant signs.

▶ *Direct obstruction of the work of God*
The girl with a spirit of divination obstructed the work of God (Acts 16:16–18). Even though she was apparently speaking truth, Paul was disturbed by her behavior and commanded the spirit to come out of her. Spirits in people who encountered Jesus called out his name in an attempt to gain power over him (Mark 1:23–27; 5:7).

I have observed the presence of spirits in mockery, inappropriate laughter, compulsive talking and distraction, for example when someone is receiving counseling or healing prayer and the evil spirit is seeking to obstruct this.

Spirits in people will stir up irrational opposition to godly people or good projects, often for no apparent reason. They will inexplicably and repeatedly spoil relationships involving leading or sensitive Christians.

If we believe with Paul that our real struggle is not with human factors but with hidden spiritual powers (Ephesians 6:12) then it is helpful before any church council or similar meeting, worship service or counseling session, to use our Christian authority to forbid any disturbance by enemy spirits.

I have found it effective in my personal prayers (i.e., not publicly) to forbid Satan or his spirits to speak through anyone. I then entrust the meeting firmly to the sole direction of the Holy Spirit and this is where I concentrate my prayers. We must not give Satan or his spirits undue attention; we address them only to rebuke them.

▶ *Paranormal phenomena*
In my judgment phenomena such as oppressed or "haunted" houses and inexplicable movements of objects, doors and windows, indicate spirits affecting the house. My experience

suggests that the spirit powers operating may relate primarily either to the place or to the people living there. In either case sin past or present must be confessed and renounced as well as deliverance from the spirits in both the person and the place.

▶ *Blatant evil or immoral practice*
Since deliberate and serious sin opens the door to the entry of spirits, the knowledge of evil practices in someone's life is a fairly sure guide.

▶ *A person's countenance*
On several occasions I have seen the presence of a spirit in a person's face, looking at their countenance with my natural sight. I see the face obviously not as God wants it to be. It is not pain, which can also often be seen in the people's faces, but rather a distortion of what I believe to be the true countenance.

This needs great care lest normal fear or a similar emotion be attributed to a spirit. It is possible, however, to see evil in a person's eyes; a false smile can be another indication.

▶ *Reaction to a command to the spirit to make itself known*
A Christian needing to know of the presence, or otherwise, of a spirit in a person they are counseling may command any spirit present in the name of Jesus Christ to make its presence known. Clear indications are then quite frequently received, for example, in involuntary body movements, or pain.

Illnesses and disorders which do not yield to treatment
I have once experienced a spirit-driven sickness as a mild stomach disorder. Unlike normal stomach "bugs" this condition appeared to have no lifespan and did not follow the usual pattern for an infection. Since the condition started after an encounter when I thought I had disobeyed God, I suspected that I had picked up a spirit and asked someone with discernment to pray for me. They discerned what it was and released me. The stomach condition was immediately cured.

I have known a case where deafness was brought on by a

spirit. I was not expecting any such cause but as soon as I put my finger gently in the person's ears and prayed for healing there was an immediate manifestation of demons.

It is not easy to discern where a mental illness is affected by the presence of a spirit. I prayed for a woman who had been diagnosed a year earlier with clinical depression. Treatment was making little headway. Looking at her countenance I sensed the need for deliverance, so I explored her story. As a missionary in Nepal she had watched a witchcraft ceremony involving the killing of a cockerel. I addressed these spirits and her body shook as they left. There were spirits also relating to rape and a dominant grandparent. She says that all has been well since the prayer time.

But I am certainly not saying that all disease is caused by a spirit. It is when the normal treatments do not yield the expected results that there is reason to look for another explanation.

Clues from a person's present experience and attitudes

In the following examples, the presence of a spirit was indicated by what a person shared about his or her experience.

- **Persistent experience of inner darkness.** This may include spiritual confusion, willful pursuing of heretical beliefs, difficulty in receiving basic Christian truth, and/or persistent blocking of commitment to Jesus. It must be discerned whether these experiences are normal doubts, or whether there is a spirit causing them.

  The god of this age has blinded the minds of unbelievers, so that they cannot see the light of the gospel of the glory of Christ, who is the image of God.   (2 Corinthians 4:4)

- **Marked blockages in normal personality or spiritual development.** Some people become emotionally stuck in childhood, as parental attitudes prevent them from growing up. A "spirit of a little child" holds them. They are then unable to grow satisfactorily through normal learning experiences into adult behavior. In a similar way when someone does not seem to grow spiritually through the normal channels of the Word, sacraments and prayer, there may be a spirit blocking this development.

- **Immovable bondage to temptation and sin** such that real attempts at repentance appear to make no impression on the problems and may involve the areas of sexual lust, deviant sexual practice (possibly including both oral and anal sex), criticism, unbelief, unforgiveness, bitterness, anger and deceit.

- **Irrational fears or phobias** which do not respond to facing up to them and seeking to overcome them.

- **Overwhelming guilt and self-condemnation** (see 1 John 19–24).

- **Irrational dislike of God's ministers**, or feeling persecuted by them. Conversely, it is a sign of a spirit to be drawn instinctively to associate with people who have occult connections.

- **A strong sense of the presence of dead relatives.** If this is a spirit, and not just the wishful thinking of the bereaved person, then opinions differ as to whether or not it is the spirit of the person which for some reason (usually death in disturbing circumstances) has not reached its final destination. If this is the case, a simple committal of the person's spirit to the mercy of God and to Christ will bring freedom. Alternatively, however, the sense of the presence of the dead may be because of an evil spirit which was attached to the dead person and is now seeking to transfer its power. The experience is a common one and I have come to the view that either explanation may be correct.

Other conditions of disorder in family members are related by Dr Kenneth McAll to the unquiet discarnate spirits of dead relatives (see his book *Healing the Family Tree*, especially chapter 3). Release is found to occur through a celebration of Holy Communion with the "family tree" placed on the altar. I have personally found this to bring marked release in some cases. However, since faith and Christ's authority are what is needed for effective deliverance, I believe that equally effective results are obtained by prayer which commands release from any spirit presence associated with the dead relative.

- **A sense of fatalism:** "What will be, will be." This attitude is strangely common and is a satanic lie to suggest that what will happen to us is already fixed. The plan of God for our lives is reshaped daily in the light of our response to him. If we believe something is inevitable we give it power and can even allow disaster into our lives. It is far better to hold on only to God's promises as certain to happen.

- **Repeated choice of black**, for example in clothing or color of car. Markedly unrestful color schemes or patterns for dress or house décor are another clue.

- **Addiction**, for example drugs, alcohol, smoking, gambling, eating, or any compulsive activity.

- **Anorexia**, I believe, usually involves a destructive spirit (its recovery rate is only about 50 per cent). As for many conditions with their roots in prenatal or childhood rejection, insecurity or bad relationships, there is great need for emotional healing of hurts and relationships. While deliverance may well be part of the ministry, emotional healing is fundamental. When those who have caused the hurt have been forgiven (this should be spoken out) and wrong attitudes of resentment or hatred confessed, the healing often comes and the spirits leave because they no longer have any right to be there.

I have learned the hard way that prayer of deliverance with anorexic persons needs great care. It is important to work with a person's consultant or doctor. When the body has suffered severe loss of weight, it may not physically be able to cope with the rush of power from the Holy Spirit and whatever impact this has on the body chemistry. On one occasion someone who was restful and quiet in a hospital bed when I prayed for her, then went into a trance and, for a brief period, failed to recognize members of her family. In God's goodness, she made a full recovery, but what happened took me by surprise and, understandably, gave me difficulty with the hospital staff.

Case histories

Careful questions about a person's history can provide important clues to the presence of evil spirits. These uncover areas which the person might not think to share unless asked the appropriate question. It is important to ask about a person's relatives and ancestry as well as about themselves.

The following are of particular significance to note in the person or their relatives.

- **Any occult practice:** Since spirits travel down inheritance channels until they are driven out, occult experiences of parents, grandparents or relatives are important clues.

- **Experiences of evil**, such as in rooms or buildings, or in shaking someone's hands, in unexpectedly seeing faces. Such experiences are quite common.

- **Striking cases of disease** or patterns of disorder repeating down the generations. See the example of Frances in Chapter 1. Some people are "accident prone" in a way that gives rise to suspicion about the involvement of spirits.

- **The community (or national) history** into which the person was born and brought up.

- **Traumatic experiences.**

- **Experience of rejection** – from the start of pregnancy in the womb, in being placed for adoption, in childhood, or later on.

- **Miscarriage or abortion.** In the case of attempted abortion, spirits of rejection, murder and death are likely. There is a view that a spirit joined to a lost child (miscarriage or abortion) can transfer to the next pregnancy and enter the next child. Whatever the explanation, prayer to release someone from the spirit of the preceding "child" seems to be effective.

- **Involvement in religious cults or sects** which deny that Jesus is the true God and died for our sins. There are similar dangers from the practice of Transcendental Meditation and some forms of Yoga where the mind is opened to influences which are not identified as Jesus and the Holy Spirit of God.

- **Dysfunctional or oppressive family features** or internalized attitudes: for example, domination, usually by a parent or grandparent. This can allow entry to spirits of control. The rejection of women (misogyny) is another significant feature of some families.

- **Use of certain alternative medicines,** for example, homoeopathy or acupuncture. It is where these treatments are associated with an unspecified life force or an astrological pattern that the danger comes. There is openness to spiritual powers other than the Holy Spirit of God.

I emphasize again that these are only clues to possible spirit presence. It should not be assumed that these circumstances always indicate the presence of spirits.

Discernment by spiritual gifts

Those who are learning to receive indications from God through the mind, the imagination, the body, or indeed any of the senses, will be shown the presence of spirits through these varied ways in which the Spirit communicates. Through a very clear dream God showed me that a particular person was under a curse. As well as seeing spirits in the countenance of people, I have on one occasion seen a demon in the form of a strikingly white death-mask covering someone's face. Clearly this was not apparent to other people or the person concerned would have been rushed to hospital.

It is possible to learn both to hear God's voice (usually in our thoughts rather than aloud) and to see what his Spirit shows us. The first step is to believe that this is not only possible, but likely! The life of Jesus and the Acts of the Apostles are full of examples of God's direct communication of knowledge or guidance to his servants.

There often remains a degree of uncertainty about the presence, or otherwise, of a spirit. This should be accepted as a commonplace aspect of warfare – just as in a battle where there may remain uncertainty about the enemy's whereabouts.

In a society which is unsettled at the thought that spirits might exist at all, this lack of certainty is difficult to handle, so many advise that spirits should only be diagnosed with great caution and as a last resort. In societies which are more relaxed about the possibility of evil spirits and where it is recognized that most of them are not very powerful, such advice is less necessary.

5

Driving out evil spirits

Jesus continues his work through us, giving us authority to drive out spirits in his name, just as the first disciples did. It is really very simple: we address the spirit – specifying what sort of spirit it is if we know (it is not always necessary to know) – and command it to leave in the name of Jesus Christ.

The fact that the spirit does not always leave immediately reminds us that this is a spiritual battle between two kingdoms. It is indeed a power struggle. We need to know, therefore, where our resources in Christ are to be found, and how to draw upon the authority and power that is available to us. We also need to understand the reasons why spirits do not leave when commanded to do so.

The importance of right theology

The spiritual battle involved in deliverance has many aspects. At the heart of it all is faith, a firm trust in God, which opens the way for God to work his blessings in our lives.

We can earn none of God's gifts. They are received in faith and gratitude. Faith in God is nourished by taking in the truth about God. St. John writes, *"You will know the truth, and the truth will set you free"* (John 8:32). It is important to be sure of the truth if the battles of deliverance are to be won.

God and Satan

When Satan (one of God's angels) rebelled, he was thrown down to earth and his angels with him. His authority in heaven was removed but he has been allowed power on earth to lead the world astray (Revelation 12:7–9, 17). Eventually Satan and his angels are destined for the *"eternal fire"* (Matthew 25:41; Revelation 20:10).

Fallen humanity

The first human beings gave authority to the serpent, believing him and doubting God (Genesis 3:1–19). In so doing they put themselves in subservience to Satan, since the serpent is Satan (Revelation 12:9).

The Genesis passages, even without a literal reading, describe the truth about how human sin has enabled Satan's present hold in the world. Human beings lost their dominion over the earth, so childbearing, relationships between men and women, and working the earth all became riddled with pain and struggle (Genesis 1:26; 3:16–19).

Jesus

Jesus was born and died completely sinless (Hebrews 4:15). His perfect obedience to God put him in a position over Satan, not under him. He was the Second Adam, the pioneer of restored human beings. The demons recognized him as *"the Holy One of God."* They knew he had authority in himself to destroy them (Mark 1:24).

Jesus, therefore, threw out evil spirits with his own authority. This was quite different from anything before it and had the crowds gasping (Mark 1:27).

Through his obedient death on the cross, Jesus made a perfect offering for sin. He stood in the place of sinful human beings under God's judgment. Satan cannot bring any valid accusations against those who trust in Jesus' sacrificial death. *"Now the prince of this world will be driven out,"* Jesus said, as he approached the cross (John 12:31).

The same victory of Jesus over the powers set against us is clear in St. Paul's letter to the Colossians:

> *God made you alive with Christ. He forgave us all our sins, having cancelled the written code, with all its regulations, that*

was against us and that stood opposed to us; he took it away, nailing it to the cross. And having disarmed the powers and authorities, he made a public spectacle of them, triumphing over them by the cross. (Colossians 2:13–15)

When God raised Jesus from being dead, he clearly proved him to be the Messiah, the ruler over sin and death. All who believe in him through faith now share in his divine life.

The people of the new order

The Messiah was long promised as the one God would send to set his people free from sin. Israel's calling to bring blessings to the whole world is now fulfilled in Jesus and his people.

Through faith in Jesus, believers now have authority to proclaim the good news, and in his name, to heal the sick and throw out evil spirits. The age of resurrection has begun. Death no longer rules, but divine life, found in Christ. For the people of Jesus, eternity is certain. The presence of the Holy Spirit with us now is a "down payment" of what will one day be our full inheritance with Christ in heaven.

Finally, God must complete his purposes so that sin and evil are completely destroyed. The return of Christ and the final Day of the Lord are certain. The kingdom of God will come. The new creation will be complete.

As the Church, the people of Christ, witness to the ultimate purpose of God, so the ministries of healing and deliverance are signs of what is to come. They are also clear expressions of God's compassion in the here and now.

Christian believers are God's priesthood. Linking earth and heaven, we are called to be channels through whom God's kingdom blessings flow freely to his world.

A biblical example of deliverance

They went to Capernaum, and when the Sabbath came, Jesus went into the synagogue and began to teach. The people were

*amazed at his teaching, because he taught them as one who had
authority, not as the teachers of the law. Just then a man in their
synagogue who was possessed by an evil spirit cried out, "What
do you want with us, Jesus of Nazareth? Have you come to
destroy us? I know who you are – the Holy One of God!"*

*"Be quiet!" said Jesus sternly. "Come out of him!" The evil
spirit shook the man violently and came out of him with a
shriek.*

*The people were all so amazed that they asked each other,
"What is this? A new teaching – and with authority! He even
gives orders to evil spirits and they obey him." News about him
spread quickly over the whole region of Galilee.*

(Mark 1:21–28)

Reference has been made several times to Mark's account of
the deliverance of the man in the synagogue. This passage is
particularly instructive for approaching prayer for deliverance.
Here are some significant points to note:

- As stated earlier, while many translations use the strong
  phrase *"a man possessed by an evil spirit,"* the Greek is more
  accurately translated as *"a man **with** an unclean spirit"* or
  even *"a man **in** an unclean spirit."*

- Both singular and plural words are used to describe the
  spirits. *"Have you come to destroy us? I know who you are."*
  This indicates several spirits, but one in charge.

- The spirit starts the contest, using Jesus' name *"the Holy
  One"* to try to gain power over Jesus.

- Jesus has indeed come to destroy them. He says *"Be quiet!"*
  or more literally, *"be throttled!"* Then he says *"Come out of
  him!"* The spirit is not sent to any place. It will go to the
  eternal fire, eventually.

- Jesus just throws it out. There is noise and some dramatic
  manifestations. There is also evangelistic impact, as the
  news of Jesus' power and authority spreads rapidly over
  the region.

Some cautions about the ministry of deliverance

The need for care and good advice

Whereas most of the world is convinced that evil spirits are real, this is not so in Western culture. More recently, much attention has been called to the possibility of abuse in a variety of ways; so in an unsympathetic culture towards the model of deliverance, mistakes are heavily punished.

Our society is becoming quick to attach blame and more litigious. In part, this is the result of losing the sense of God's providence over all things. He is no longer regarded as the first point of help in a difficulty: the one who allowed the situation to happen and to whom we must turn for help. If God is out of the picture, when disaster happens people have no alternative from blaming themselves other than blaming others.

For these reasons extra care needs to be taken in prayer for deliverance. Here are some guidelines.

- Do nothing that even remotely violates a person's dignity.

- Have other witnesses present.

- Proceed slowly, securing the person's full agreement for what seems to be the most appropriate way to pray.

- When a person is under professional care, work with the professionals concerned.

- Ask a doctor to advise and, if any difficulty is expected, to be present.

- Follow carefully the guidelines for such ministry issued by your local and national church.

Principal keys to effective deliverance

Be filled with the Holy Spirit's power

Since deliverance is a power struggle we need not only to know the authority we have been given but also the power of God moving through us. The authority is fixed and given in principle to all Christians, since all are disciples. (Churches, however, have their own patterns for authorizing ministry which need to be respected.) The power of God, on the other hand, varies in its presence and we must learn to seek it.

Jesus gave his followers both power and authority to do this ministry as they traveled the country proclaiming the kingdom of God (Luke 9:1). Powerful deliverance ministry flows from a powerful prayer life. Some spirits only come out after prayer and, perhaps, fasting (Mark 9:29).

Discern the evil spirit's "right" to be there and deal with the sin

A vital factor in driving out evil spirits is to discover what gives them their opportunity to be there in the first place. Satan has no right over those who are God's, except where sin has not been confessed and dealt with.

Where sin has allowed a foothold, this must be confessed in the presence of another Christian (James 5:16). Often there is reluctance to do this because of shame about a particular sin; common examples are sexual acts outside marriage, lustful acts or holding unforgiveness towards someone. The way forward may be confession privately to someone in the team of the same sex before the deliverance prayer goes ahead.

This indicates the importance of working in teams, men and women together. Deliverance ministry should not normally be attempted on one's own; having someone else present provides protection both physically and as a witness to what is said and done. With more powerful spirits a larger team is advisable.

As described in Chapter 4, the sin which gives the spirit the right to be present may be primarily voluntary – of the person's own will. Alternatively, it may be involuntary, originating in a person's forebears or some other person towards the person concerned. Sometimes people have great difficulty in speaking of the hurt or abuse caused to them. They need to be assured that we are not concerned to blame but only in bringing the truth to light, so that there may be full forgiveness expressed and the spirit identified so as to be driven out. Sometimes the pain is so great that it has to be unfolded gradually.

More difficult to shift are the spirits passed down relating to sins from several generations back. A complex weave of sins can be built up over several generations and there can be multiple spirit presence. The nature of the spirits will be seen in the problems encountered by the person, but not always very clearly, and what originally gave them right of entry into the family line is not always easy to discover.

It is helpful, and sometimes essential, to receive knowledge direct from God about the sin at the point of entry. Every church seeking to practice deliverance ministry therefore needs to learn to receive through the Holy Spirit what are called *"words of knowledge"* or a *"message of knowledge"* (see 1 Corinthians 12:8). One example of Jesus using such a word of knowledge is in John 4:18.

In our experience, over the course of time some team members learn to hear remarkable words of knowledge very accurately. However, great care and wisdom need to be exercised until such words are confirmed, lest damage be done, for example by inappropriately putting a slur on a family's reputation.

If there is difficulty in discerning the point of entry it may be necessary to return to the ministry on another occasion after further prayer. Some deliverance ministry takes time and several sessions. God honors our perseverance and leads us on step by step. There is no short cut to learning other than by experience.

In preparation for deliverance, the person seeking ministry should:

- Confess all known personal sins and ask for God's forgiveness.

- Renounce all occult involvement (either their own or their ancestors'), including any possible witchcraft, Satanism or Freemasonry.

- Ask God to have mercy on those in previous generations who gave Satan opportunity to enter through sin (acknowledging that we, too, are sinners).

- Speak out forgiveness to all who have caused hurt and against whom they have harbored bitterness, resentment or hatred. This should also be towards forbears for actions which have caused spiritual bondage to the present day. It is important to speak words blessing those who did wrong (Luke 6:28; Romans 12:14).

- Confess Jesus Christ as the Son of God, and their personal Savior from sin. Declare that Jesus Christ is made Lord over every aspect of their life. This is the supreme goal for every believer's life and the key to complete deliverance from the enemy's hold.

- Renounce any spirit believed to be present.

- A prayer of protection may also be appropriate.

- Command the spirit to leave in Jesus' name.

The ground of victory lies solely with what Jesus has accomplished. It is powerful to proclaim this confidently as the ministry proceeds. The words used in prayer can helpfully stress the following:

- the sinlessness of Jesus, the Holy One

- the sacrificial work of Jesus on the cross; his blood that dealt with sin and thereby destroyed the accuser's weapons

- the name of Jesus – to which every knee will bow

- the kingdom or rule of God which Jesus has established

- God's praise. This is effective because it expresses God's rule and therefore overthrows the rule of the enemy. Satan and his spirits hate the worship of God.

It is important that one person is in charge of the prayer, even if the authority is passed to others at certain times. Team members should respect the leader's authority.

Remind the demon of the authority you have in Jesus Christ and command it to leave in the name of Jesus. Frequently, but not always, there will be at least mild manifestations in the person's body, signs of a struggle or of a spirit leaving. Coughing is common and vomiting occurs on occasions.

Most spirits leave through the mouth, while some leave in the way they came, for example, through the eyes, the sexual orifices, or the fingers. They hold on to parts of the body (the person being set free is often aware of this), and this hold can be released in Jesus' name. The spirits deceive and may appear to have gone when they have not.

Deliverance does not need noise; it needs faith in God, in the authority he has committed to us, and in the power of the Spirit. I tend to raise my voice a bit in order to take confidence and act as someone commanding the intruder to leave. But noise is not necessary and can be distracting, frightening, or simply a sign that our faith is weak. If we want this ministry to be treated as routine and undramatic, we need to be as matter-of-fact and quietly firm about it as possible.

It can be helpful to command the spirits not to hurt anyone or to make a noise. The release of deep emotional pain, however, is easily confused with the cries of a spirit.

On occasions it is better not to use words like "demon" or "spirit." Our team ministered to a Christian who also told fortunes. She was quite unable to cope with the notion that evil spirits were operating in her. "I am a good person," she insisted. More judicious words should have been used by the team. If there was confession and repentance, probably a quiet prayer to send any darkness or power away would have been sufficient. A lot of deliverance happens without mention of spirits!

The person seeking deliverance should be encouraged to be an active participant in expelling the spirit. Calling on Jesus for help may be necessary. It can also be helpful to breathe in the Holy Spirit – taking in a deep breath with the intention of receiving the Spirit, then expelling the demon, coughing and breathing it out.

No method should be used which violates the dignity of the person. Long and protracted sessions should also be avoided: there can be a break for a drink and a rest.

At the end of the ministry the place occupied by the evil spirits must be filled with the Holy Spirit, usually with laying on of hands. I commit the person to God's care, asking that, where further ministry is needed, the Holy Spirit will prepare the person, bringing to light what we need to know.

"How do you know when the spirits have gone?"

You do not always know and sometimes you have to believe this by faith. In due course it becomes clear if the problem they created is cleared. Often, however, the person knows that the spirit has gone, the manifestations cease, or you yourself know inwardly.

Some say that demons should be sent to the lake of fire or to report to Jesus. I am content just to command them depart, as Jesus did. As Twelftree shows, Jesus understood deliverance to be in two stages; at the first stage the demon leaves the person, the second is the final defeat of Satan and his demons at the last judgment. Since all demons will go ultimately to the *"lake of fire"* (Matthew 25:41; Revelation 20:10), it does no harm to remind them of this fact.

When spirits do not leave in response to our commands it is best to avoid prolonging the ministry by endlessly repeating what you have already done. Instead look further at:

- Occult practices that have not been confessed, renounced and dealt with

- Sin that has not been confessed or even if confessed, not truly repented of

- Sin by ancestors (a family tree may be helpful indicating patterns of disorder or death in unnatural circumstances); words of knowledge may be needed

- Lack of will to be set free

- Lack of faith that Christ has brought about complete freedom

- An unhealthy bond to a person (possibly a dead person)

• The possibility of an incorrect diagnosis. The problem may not lie with a spirit at all.

Further prayer, listening to God, and perhaps fasting, may be called for. In *Christian, Set Yourself Free*, Graham Powell describes how after many years of torment his own deliverance came through taking a clear position of faith that Christ had set him free from the evil spirits in him. He then took authority over them commanding them to go in the name of Christ. Many times before this, well-meaning Christian ministers, after failing to accomplish the deliverance then told him that there were no evil spirits in him.

I have found personally that the effectiveness of my prayers for deliverance has increased as two convictions have deepened within me: the first, of **the immense power of the Holy Spirit;** the second, **a holy anger at the presence of such intruders in the lives of God's created people.**

Pray for protection if necessary
Most people are afraid when first setting out on this ministry and then a prayer of protection is wise:

"We claim the protection of the blood of Jesus over each person here, our families, our church families, and over all the possessions God has given us to steward."

Although fear is understandable, is nevertheless not God's best for us and it gives Satan opportunity. While the prayer of protection guards against this, it is better still not to be afraid.

Jesus has transferred us from the kingdom of darkness to his own kingdom (Colossians 1:13) and we are secure and fully protected in him. There is nothing to fear, as he repeatedly told his disciples. We are completely loved by God and given authority for this ministry. When we are sure of our standing in Christ we will not find it so necessary to ask specially for protection; indeed quite a lot of concern to do this comes from fear rather than from faith.

The importance of working under authority

One of the problems in the Church of England is that prayer for deliverance is not yet accepted as routine prayer. The presence of evil spirits is treated as a rare phenomenon requiring great caution. In many dioceses no deliverance ministry is to be attempted without reference to the bishop or whoever he designates. This is impractical if spirits are widespread and mostly not very powerful (such as those I earlier describe having picked up).

In *Deliverance*, Michael Perry draws a distinction between a lesser exorcism, prayers asking for deliverance, and a greater exorcism involving a direct command to the demon or demonic forces. He argues that only for the greater exorcism is the bishop's permission necessary. This seems unsatisfactory, however, if Jesus is our model, since he dealt with all spirits by command.

If you work in a Church such as Anglican or Roman Catholic, where you are under wider authority, I suggest you look for an agreement with your bishop that you consult with him only over any case which looks serious and has the feel of a major deliverance about it. Nevertheless, in handling the smaller stuff locally, you and other members of your team must work under a careful authority structure in the local church.

In conclusion, it is important that anyone who practices this ministry should do so under the proper authority of their minister who himself or herself should be under the proper authority established in that church.

6

After deliverance

It cannot be emphasized too strongly that our ministry is to people and not to spirits. God is looking for a faith which believes firmly in Christ and holds to his promises; he is looking for a resolute will to choose good thoughts and actions; he is looking for people who within the fellowship of the church will obey him and move in the power of the Holy Spirit. The ministry of deliverance has a place, but is only one part in the much greater context of growing as a Christian. When a person's will is weak, or their faith shallow, deliverance will be difficult to sustain. It requires good soil to resist sin and Satan and for the word of Christ to bear fruit. In many cases a lot of work has to be done building good foundations of faith in Christ and a resolute will before deliverance will be complete.

Some people will come back again and again for deliverance, when what they need is discipline in their thoughts, aligning their minds with Scripture and choosing to believe what God says is true and not what their feelings, or imagination, are saying. A successful deliverance ministry in the more complex cases will proceed step by step with a program of faith building. This may happen through the fellowship groups of the church, personal study of the Bible and prayer, and one-to-one nurture by experienced leaders.

The rebuilding of the will in a weak-willed person is much the more difficult task than the prayer for deliverance. It means helping the person to have manageable goals which they can achieve, thereby giving them confidence. As they grow, the targets can become more stretching. Only as the will becomes strong can the person possibly choose for themselves the right attitudes and actions necessary to resist Satan. Living in a supportive community will help.

It is helpful to teach those receiving deliverance ministry to move forward in the following ways:

1. **Accept firmly that as believers who are *"in Christ,"* they are secure and protected.** Satan cannot harm them.

2. **Be strongly on guard against temptation to sin,** and especially in thoughts such as those of self-rejection or self-hatred, or of unforgiveness or anger towards others.

3. **Stick closely with Christians** while the old patterns of thoughts or actions are broken.

4. **Learn Scripture** and use it to combat the lies which Satan feeds into our thoughts.

5. **When the conflict is strong, call upon Jesus for help** and for the Holy Spirit's presence to fill them daily.

6. **Drive Satan away:** "In the name of Jesus go from me, Satan. I serve Jesus as Lord and belong to him."

Following deliverance ministry a person may well feel tired and weak. They may feel the loss of their former identity as a person, if the spirits pressed in hard on their attitudes. It will take time for them to find their new identity as the person God intended them to be. It is important to support them with plenty of love and help in this period and to let their stability develop before they are asked to share their testimony.

7

Causes for concern about this ministry

Since the ministry of deliverance from evil spirits is foreign to our Western culture, it is not surprising that it easily arouses concern. I believe that all such concern needs to be considered carefully.

This chapter is not short because I think that there are few grounds for concern. My hope is rather that in the preceding chapters my response to many legitimate objections has been clarified. I offer in addition my response to three common grounds for concern.

► *Belief in evil spirits is a way of evading personal responsibility for evil and is therefore an unhelpful model.*

Experience in this ministry soon bears out that people only get free of evil spirits if they exercise full responsibility and with all their strength of will turn away from what is wrong. So in no way is full personal responsibility side-stepped. We have already indicated that it is sin alone which gives Satan's spirits any right to be present; deliverance therefore requires firm repentance as well as confession and forgiveness. Work is often necessary to help someone to face this responsibility before deliverance can be accomplished and sustained.

► *Belief in evil spirits fosters a superstitious and primitive approach to the world.*

Most of the world is convinced that evil spirits exist and we need to be open to the possibility that this is accurate. With right teaching this can be handled quite factually and without creating an aura of superstition.

Belief in evil spirits need not be in conflict with the truth discovered in psychology or medicine as the explanations offered are not necessarily mutually exclusive. They can be complementary. Believing that someone has a demon does not mean believing that they do not need psychiatric help. I look forward to constructive participation in working together for people's health.

▶   *Deliverance ministry is dangerous and has been known to be*
     followed by suicide or violent crime.

Wherever people are under professional care for their condition I have made a rule always to work in consultation with their psychiatrist, physician, counselor or social worker. It is important not to disrupt the existing pattern of treatment. Furthermore, a mistake in the ministry of deliverance can lead to justified condemnation for a ministry that is unprofessional.

When people are under professional psychiatric care, the personality is often seriously disturbed and is not such as to provide the firm basis of repentance and faith necessary for effective deliverance. In this sort of case it may not be appropriate to proceed at all with deliverance ministry. Certainly, it is vital to proceed with great caution in the partnership already emphasized.

If deliverance ministry with more stable people is practiced under firm leadership and authority in the local church it will ensure that potentially difficult cases are treated with responsibility and wisdom. During my time as Vicar of Holy Trinity, Coventry we had two doctors as members of our ministry team and we involved them in such cases.

A prayer that can be prayed at any time is simply: "Your kingdom, Lord, in my friend." The kingdom is God's rule of order and wholeness and love. It is how Jesus taught us to pray. We can pray the kingdom into any person, institution, nation or church: "Your kingdom come. Your will be done on earth, as in heaven." This prayer will prepare the ground for possible healing and deliverance ministry later.

If you have enjoyed this book and would like to help us to send a copy of it and many other titles to needy pastors in the **Third World,** please write for further information or send your gift to:

**Sovereign World Trust
PO Box 777, Tonbridge
Kent TN11 0ZS
United Kingdom**

or to the **'Sovereign World'** distributor in your country.

Visit our website at **www.sovereign-world.org** for a full range of Sovereign World books.